ideals®

MOTHER'S DAY

This is a day for mothers,
   Just one day set apart,
A time above all others,
   To gladden a mother's heart,

With something to garnish the trying days
   That are scattered throughout the years,
When Mother's smiles and Mother's ways
   Banished our childhood tears.

But how can I add to the laurels,
   In thought, in word or line;
How can I repay your love
   And your tenderness, Mother of mine.

I would that the thoughts recalled today,
   Might someway be expressed;
The memories within my heart,
   The thoughts I hold as best.

Of recollections cherished most,
   No sweeter thoughts could be
Than those of you, my Mother,
   Inscribed in memory.

Frank D. Felt

Editorial Director, James Kuse
Managing Editor, Ralph Luedtke
Associate Editor, Colleen Callahan Gonring
Production Editor/Manager, Richard Lawson
Photographic Editor, Gerald Koser
Contributing Editors, Beverly Rae Wiersum
                       Judy A. Turck

Mother's Garden

Joy Belle Burgess

All along her pleasant way
Mother walked among her flowers;
And deep within the sun and shade,
She found a peace to fill her hours.
The soft pink garlands of the rose
Enriched the air with sweet perfume,
While murmurings of honeybees
Drifted from each flower bloom.

All along her pleasant way
Her paths were dream-beguiled,
Down pillared aisles of hollyhocks
And in amongst the daisies' smiles;
While butterflies on graceful wing
Mingled with her garden's gems,
And flitted o'er the brightest blooms
In the maze of leaves and stems.

All along her pleasant way
She walked in peace, alone, apart,
And found beyond the garden gate
A sanctuary for her heart.

An Old-Fashioned Garden

Carice Williams

How pleasant to remember
The joys of yesteryear,
A sweet old-fashioned garden
That Mother held so dear.

Baby's breath of pure white
Edged many a flower bed
Where pinks and larkspurs, pansies too,
Held high each pretty head.

Each flower in Mother's garden
Was treated with such care,
As though they were her children,
Entrusted to her care.

These days, old-fashioned gardens
Are very, very few;
What joy 'twould be to walk once more
Where sweet primroses grew!

When gardens start awakening
As spring returns once more,
I see my Mother's garden
Through mem'ry's open door.

ISBN 0-89542-323-5 295

IDEALS—Vol. 36 No. 3, March MCMLXXIX, IDEALS is published eight times a year, January, February, March, May, July, September, November and December—
by IDEALS PUBLISHING CORPORATION, 11315 Watertown Plank Road, Milwaukee, Wis. 53226.
Second class postage paid at Milwaukee, Wisconsin. Copyright © MCMLXXIX by IDEALS PUBLISHING CORPORATION.
All rights reserved. Title IDEALS registered U.S. Patent Office.

ONE YEAR SUBSCRIPTION—eight consecutive issues as published—only $16.00
TWO YEAR SUBSCRIPTION—sixteen consecutive issues as published—only $28.00
SINGLE ISSUES—only $2.95

Photograph Oppos
Fred Sieb

The Madonna Lily

Della Crowder Miller

It came as a song in the morning,
While the dew lay fresh on the ground;
It stood like a bride in the garden
In its white satin folds, softly gowned.

It was pure and modest as Mary,
Holy Mother, the chosen, divine!
And like Mary, its sweetness lingers,
That Madonna Lily of mine.

Mary Gardens

Beverly Rae Wiersum

Centuries before the birth of Christ, people initiated the custom of surrounding their homes and arraying themselves with blossoming spring flowers in celebration of spring's victory over winter. During the Middle Ages, Christians, adopting this custom as a special way of honoring Mary, the Mother of Christ, planted "Mary gardens." Although this tradition faded out for a time, it has recently been revived in many areas of Europe and the United States. A remnant of the Mary gardens also survives in the practice of presenting mothers with bouquets of flowers on Mother's Day.

In a typical Mary garden, a statue of the Blessed Virgin occupies a place of honor, standing either in the center of the garden or in a shrine near the wall. Often complemented by a birdbath or bubbling fountain, the figure is surrounded by the flowers traditionally associated with Mary. Bell-shaped blossoms dominate, ringing out their tributes to the Madonna. Lilies of the valley, said to have sprung from Mary's tears as she wept at the foot of the cross, bear the name Our Lady's tears. Together with vivid yellow marigolds, Mary's buds, they often adorn her shrines for the Feast of the Annunciation on March 25 and during the month of May, Mary's month. The early blossoming snowdrops or snowbells, the first floral tribute of the year at Mary's shrines on Candlemas, February 2, symbolize her radiant purity. Foxgloves, with white and violet blossoms, add their dash of color to the Mary garden. Their delicate clusters of little bells prompted medieval gardeners to call them Our Lady's thimbles. Columbine, often referred to as Our Lady's shoes, are said to have sprung forth at the touch of Mary's foot.

There are still other flowers found in the Mary garden with special meanings, such as the fragrant rosemary, which blooms a pale blue. According to legend, these blooms turned from white to blue, Mary's color, in reward for the service they performed when Mary, enroute to Egypt, spread Jesus' freshly washed clothes on them to dry. Also included in a Mary garden are violets, which are tributes to Mary's humility. Although the lily is more commonly thought of to symbolize Christ's risen life, it is also known in many parts of Europe as the Madonna Lily, symbolizing the innocence, purity, and virginity of the Mother of Christ.

The crowning glory of a Mary garden, the rose, stands for the Blessed Virgin herself. White roses represent her joys, red her sufferings, and yellow her glories. And so, in a bright and joyous way, the Mary garden serves as a lovely tribute to the Mother of God's Son.

There is a sweetness at May's end that no other time of the year can equal. And by sweetness I mean more than flower fragrance or honey taste; this is the greater sweetness of understanding and emotion, the glow of pleasure in being.

This is the sensory season. Trees are in leaf and it is a green world full of elusive fragrances. Walk through an orchard and you can smell as well as feel the strength of grass underfoot, new grass reaching toward the sun. Boughs naked only a little while ago, then bright and heady with blossom, now rustle with leaf and tingle with the strength of fruition. When I pause to listen I can almost hear the flow of sap and the mysterious workings of chlorophyll.

The hills are rounded with their own green growth, the soft hills of lush and friendly land. The valleys sing with running water, valleys that have not yet felt the thirst of summer. Even the rocks are alive with vine, the creeping tendrils of life that would root in granite and suck faint sustenance from sandstone.

Hal Borland

Photograph Opposi
WASHINGTON
Ed Cooper

Phyllis C. Michael

Phyllis C. Michael was born in Berwick, Pennsylvania in 1908. It was not until the age of thirty-seven, however, that she began her literary career when, in the midst of a personal crisis, she wrote the hymn, "Take Thou My Hand." The hymn won first place in a national favorite hymns contest. Since that time, Mrs. Michael has composed music for hymns as well as written lyrics for other composers. This talented author-composer has written and published six books, as well as contributed songs, articles, and poems to many other publications, including Ideals. Mrs. Michael has received numerous awards, achieving national and international recognition. Her poems reflect her own life experiences, Mrs. Michael explains, and she hopes that through God's blessing, her words may benefit all who read them.

A Mother's Part

It's a wonderful part each mother plays
In this old world of ours;
She rules with just a kindly word
O'er the great and mighty powers.

She builds our nations large and small
With just a kindly touch,
For she builds them in the very heart
Of the child she loves so much.

All I Ask

Lord, make me all a mother should be
That I may lead my child to thee.

To Mother-in-Law

I wish Mother dear, I had known your son
When he was just a boy;
I often wonder what he was like,
What things would bring him joy.

I wish that I had seen the curls
That framed his baby face;
I wish I had seen you rock him to sleep
There on the old home place.

I wish I had heard the little prayers
You prayed as you knelt by his bed;
I know they were meant to be heard by God
But if I had heard what you said,

Perhaps I'd know why your little boy
Grew so perfect and strong and fine;
Then I could pray the same way today,
Make the same kind of man out of mine.

My Wish for You

Little daughter of mine, I'd give you the world
If it were mine to give;
I'd give you its sunbeams, its roses, its dew
To keep as long as you live.

But since it's not mine to give you these things,
There's a wish I'd wish instead,
May you have for your own, some bright golden day,
A sweet little curly head,

A daughter as fine as you've always been,
A sweet little girl of your own;
Then you'll be as happy as I am today,
You'll be a queen on her throne.

The Mother of Many

God, bless the teacher, she's the mother of many.
Who can count the moments she spends
Planning and praying for all her children,
Watching the way the twig bends?

Only a teacher can smooth life's pathway
With such a competent hand;
Only a teacher can point to the goalpost,
Implanting a vision so grand.

Only a teacher can reach out beyond her
Into the realms of youth;
Only a teacher can see her children
With the eyes of both love and truth.

Remembered Yesterdays

Garnett Ann Schultz

Oh, sweet remembered yesterdays
Along a country lane,
The times we'd walk there hand in hand
In summer sun or rain,
A quiet road with trees grown tall
All shaded from the sun,
A dream to share so real and sweet
When day at last was done.

The springtime path all edged with flowers,
The summer days serene,
Into the autumn's glowing hours
The beauties tucked between,
A singing bird along the trail
That leads into the wood,
And then the mountain reaching up,
All nature bright and good.

Oh, lovely treasured yesterdays
So beautiful to see,
To think about the happy hours
Life sent to you and me,
I lose myself in mem'ries now
For years have quickly flown,
But still my heart cannot forget
The happiness I've known.

I pause to dream—to fill my soul
With riches that I find,
A miracle before my eyes,
A peace to fill my mind.
I never tire of walking here
Along life's treasured ways,
My heart is happy as I keep
Remembered yesterdays.

Photograph Opposite
Fred Sieb

I Wish I'd Known
My Mother When . . .

Brenda Leigh

I wish I'd known my mother
    When she was just a girl.
I'm sure my father thought her
    The sweetest in the world.
I know he asked her father
    Before they set the date.
Then Mother wore her diamond
    To show that she would wait.

Mother's trousseau had to be
    A handmade work of art.
There must have been a dozen
    New suits and gowns to start.
Linens, cross-stitch, appliques,
    Fine quilts of blue and gold,
Most of all, her wedding gown
    Was lovely to behold.

I wish I had been present
    At Hillside church that day
To hear them sing "O Promise Me,"
    And brush their tears away,
To kiss the happy couple
    When it was time to go.
I wish I had been present
    With lots of rice to throw.

Their honeymoon was special.
　　They caught the westbound train.
I could have waved good-bye then,
　　And kissed them once again.
I would have asked the porter
　　To give them tender care;
I'm sure he guessed their secret
　　(The rice was in their hair.)

I know they bought a cottage
　　Just large enough for two.
My mother dusted it with love,
　　Baked sugar cookies, too.
I wish I'd been her neighbor
　　Who came for snacks and teas,
Who talked across the back fence
　　Exchanging recipes.

I recall when I was small
　　She taught me prayerfully.
Sometimes I think my mother was
　　A little bit like me.
Of all the people in the world,
　　Much more than any other,
I wish I might have known her,
　　Before she was my mother.

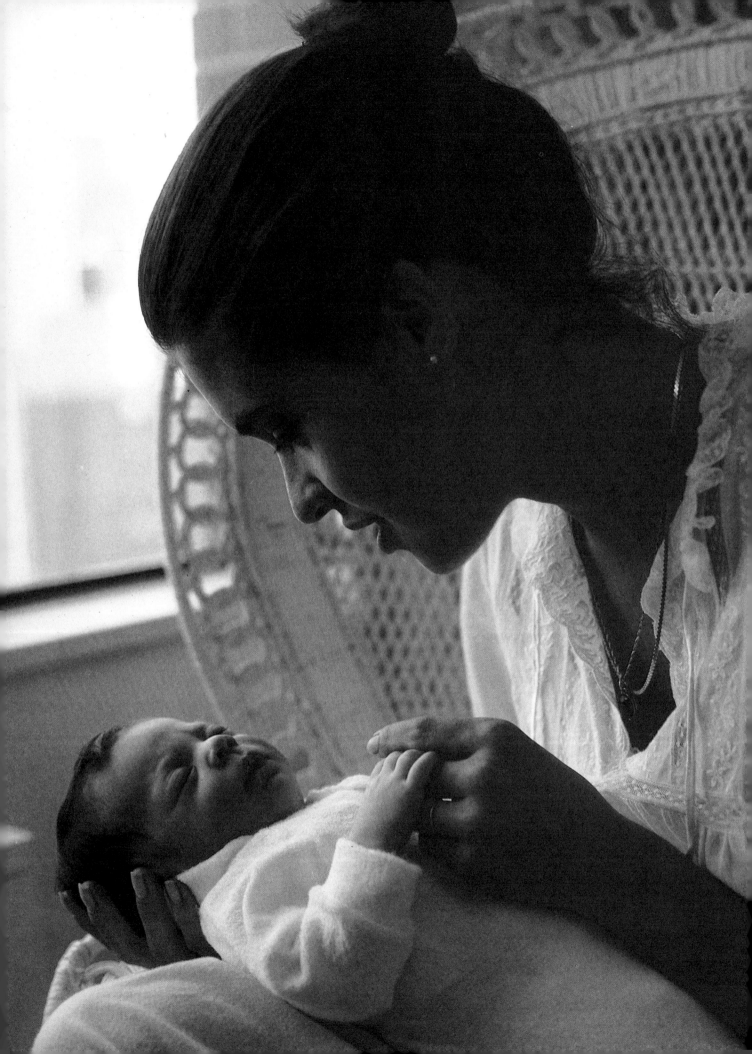

Only a Mother Knows

The wonderful feeling of joy and pride,
With her little one cuddling close;
The heavenly joy of a baby near,
Only a mother knows.

The happiness singing in her heart
With it warm against her breast;
The whispering words of love that lull
The baby dear to rest.

The tenderness of her newborn babe
With all its precious charms;
The motherly love beyond compare
For the baby in her arms.

The wonderful feeling of joy and pride,
With her little one cuddling close;
The heavenly joy of a baby near,
Only a mother knows.

Joy Belle Burgess

To a New Mother

To you, on whom the blush of youth still glows,
Your cheek, though pale, resembles still a rose,
Your eyes shine brighter, as they seem to smile,,
While in your arms, our baby rests awhile.

To you, whose patient waiting brought reward,
Your role as mother, in the play of life you've starred.
I give you love, and in our hearts' begun
A life anew, shared only with our son.

Evelyn Weeks Taylor

The History of Mother's Day

" . . . the service rendered by the American mothers is the greatest source of the country's strength and inspiration . . . "[from the congressional resolution presented by Senator Sheppherd of Texas and Congressman Heflan of Alabama].

On the second Sunday in May, mothers receive more attention than at any other time of the year. Grateful daughters and sons express their love and appreciation through special favors, cards, gifts, and flowers. In the United States this custom is a relatively recent development, only in existence since 1908. The tradition of honoring mothers, however, is a revival of a practice that dates back to the Greek empire. The ancient Greeks dedicated their annual spring festival to Rhea, the wife of Cronus and mother of the gods and goddesses.

On the Ides of March, the Romans observed this event, the Hilaria, by making offerings in the temple of Cybele, the great mother of the gods. Early Christians celebrated this festival on the fourth Sunday in Lent in honor of the Virgin Mary, the Mother of Christ. They adorned the churches with flowers, jewels, rich metals, and expensive gifts.

In England, an ecclesiastical order decreed this day as Mothering Sunday, expanding the holiday to include all mothers. Besides attending church services in honor of the Virgin Mary, children went "a-mothering," returning home from the cities with gifts, flowers, and special cakes. However, the custom of dedicating a particular day to mothers did not transfer across the ocean to the United States. No official Mother's Day existed until the twentieth century, when Anna M. Jarvis, a Philadelphia schoolteacher, began organizing a national movement for the establishment of such a day.

Anna's mother, Mrs. Anna Reese Jarvis, had originally conceived the idea of an annual, nationwide holiday honoring mothers. She believed that a day in honor of mothers could help reunite families torn apart by the bitter hatred of the Civil War. Mrs. Jarvis died on 9 May 1905, before she was able to realize her dream; however, her daughter did not abandon the idea.

Two years after her mother passed away, Anna began formulating a campaign for the national observance of a day devoted to mothers. Unmarried and alone with her blind sister Elsinore, Anna felt the loss of her mother deeply. Convinced that she, and all children, neglected to appreciate their mothers while they lived, Anna believed that a Mother's Day would increase respect for parents and strengthen home ties. Enlisting advice and

financial assistance from John Wanamaker, she wrote countless letters to people from all walks of life, including congressmen.

At Anna's request, on Sunday, 10 May 1908, the minister of the church in which Mrs. Jarvis had taught, Andrews Methodist Episcopal Church in Grafton, West Virginia, arranged a special service honoring Mrs. Jarvis. Anna donated 500 white carnations, her mother's favorite flower, to be worn by everyone in attendance. On this first official Mother's Day, the pastor used the biblical text, "Woman, behold thy son; Son, behold thy mother" (John 19:26).

The observance of Mother's Day spread quickly throughout the United States and to several foreign countries. In December 1912, the Mother's Day International Association came into existence. Finally, on May 9, 1914, President Woodrow Wilson proclaimed the second Sunday in May as Mother's Day and recognized Miss Anna Jarvis as the founder.

At first, Americans observed Mother's Day by attending the churches of their baptisms and by visiting or writing letters to their mothers. Gradually, other ways of expressing affection were added, such as giving presents and candy, mailing cards, and sending flowers. In 1934, the postal department issued a three-cent stamp of the painting of Whistler's mother as a special tribute to all mothers past and present. Today, Mother's Day offers us the opportunity to repay at least a portion of our mothers' self-sacrificing, patient, loving care, and to preserve and further develop that special, enduring relationship between mother and child.

Beverly Rae Wiersum

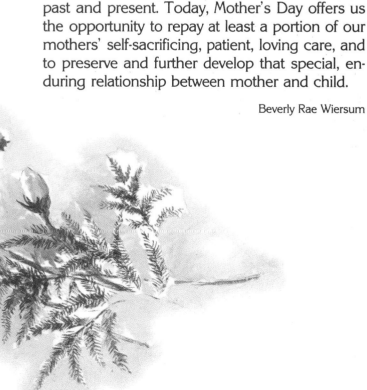

A Rose for Mother

Another Mother's Day is here,
  Bringing joy and pleasures new.
On this special day, Mother dear,
  I want to remember you.

I cannot give you costly gifts,
  And I've told you this before,
No matter what I give to you,
  You give back much, much more.

I'm giving you a pure, sweet rose,
  Gathered in the early morn,
This rose you planted in my heart
  The day that I was born.

In kindly, loving thoughts of you,
  And with the faith you still impart,
The rose I give to you today
  Is the love that's in my heart.

Cleo M. Shoffstall

Story Hour

The time of day I like the best
Is just before the hours of rest,
When twilight shadows slowly creep
And all the world prepares for sleep.
When daily tasks and chores are through,
And I may spend an hour with you.

Then arm-in-arm, and hand-in-hand,
We take a trip to Story Land!
You sit enraptured, eyes aglow,
While I tell tales of long ago.
Of Goldilocks, Red Riding Hood,
And two wee babes lost in a wood.

Ere long the sandman sprinkles sand
To beckon you to Sleepy Land.
Your eyelids droop, you nod your head,
Then I must tuck you into bed.
How soon the day has passed from view,
And story hour with you is through.

Somehow I love this hour best,
And feel that I am truly blest.
What more reward has life than this,
A dearly loved child's good-night kiss?
What richer gifts can life bestow
Than joys which only mothers know?

Almeta Baka

Slumber Song

Celia Thaxter

Thou, little child, with tender clinging arms,
Drop thy sweet head, my darling, down and rest
Upon my shoulder, rest with all thy charms;
Be soothed and comforted, be loved and blessed.

Against thy silken honey-colored hair
I lean a loving cheek, a mute caress;
Close, close I gather thee and kiss thy fair
White eyelids, sleep so softly doth oppress.

Dear little face that lies in calm content
Within the gracious hollow that God made
In every human shoulder, where He meant
Some tired head for comfort should be laid.

More like a heavy, folded rose thou art
In summer air reposing. Warm and still,
Dream thy sweet dreams upon my quiet breast,
I watch thy slumber; naught shall do thee ill.

Photograph Oppos
Three Lions, Inc.

Mother's Helpers

Oh, it's cookie-making morning
   And our kitchen looks a sight.
There is flour spread on the table,
   There is flour to left and right;
There is ginger mixed with sugar
   And each spice can on the rack
Bears the fingerprints of "someone"
   Who was "going to" put it back.

There are raisins and molasses
   All in little pools around
Where some happy little fingers
   Think such morsels should be found;
There is butter on the mixer
   And on "someone's" mouth and hair,
But my darling little daughter
   Thinks she ought to "help" me there.

Oh, it's cookie-making morning
   And our kitchen looks a sight;
But what mother here among us
   Would deny her child this right?

Phyllis C. Michael

Where's Mom?

Where's Mom? There's a big raid
  On those cookies she made!
They're disappearing fast;
  They never, never last.

Where's Mom? I want to know.
  I've got something to show,
My big yellow moth
  Is ready to take off!

I want to tell Mom now,
  That she may take a bow,
My new jacket she made
  Puts others in the shade!

When I was sick in bed,
  I liked it when she read
Stories of dragons and knights,
  'Cause she acted stuff out just right!

And when I cut my knee,
  Mom bandaged it and kissed me;
For better or for worse,
  She should have been a nurse.

Where's Mom? Sometimes at night,
  She comes in and turns on the light
When I've had a bad dream,
  And things aren't what they seem.

Hey Mom, before I run out the door,
  I want to say one thing more,
"Who's got the best Mom?" I say,
  "I do!" Happy Mother's Day!

Maurine Wagner

Definition

Grace Noll Crowell

I search among the plain and lovely words
To find what the one word "mother" means;
As well try to define the tangled song of birds;
The echo in the hills of one clear bell.

"Mother"—a word that holds the tender spell
Of all the dear essential things of earth;
A home, clean sunlit rooms, the good smell
Of bread, a table spread, a glowing hearth.
And love beyond the dream of anyone
I search for words for her, and there are none.

One cannot snare the wind, or catch the wings
Of shadows flying low across the wheat;
Ah, who can prison simple, natural things
That make the long days beautiful and sweet?

Photograph Opposite
Robert Cushman Hayes

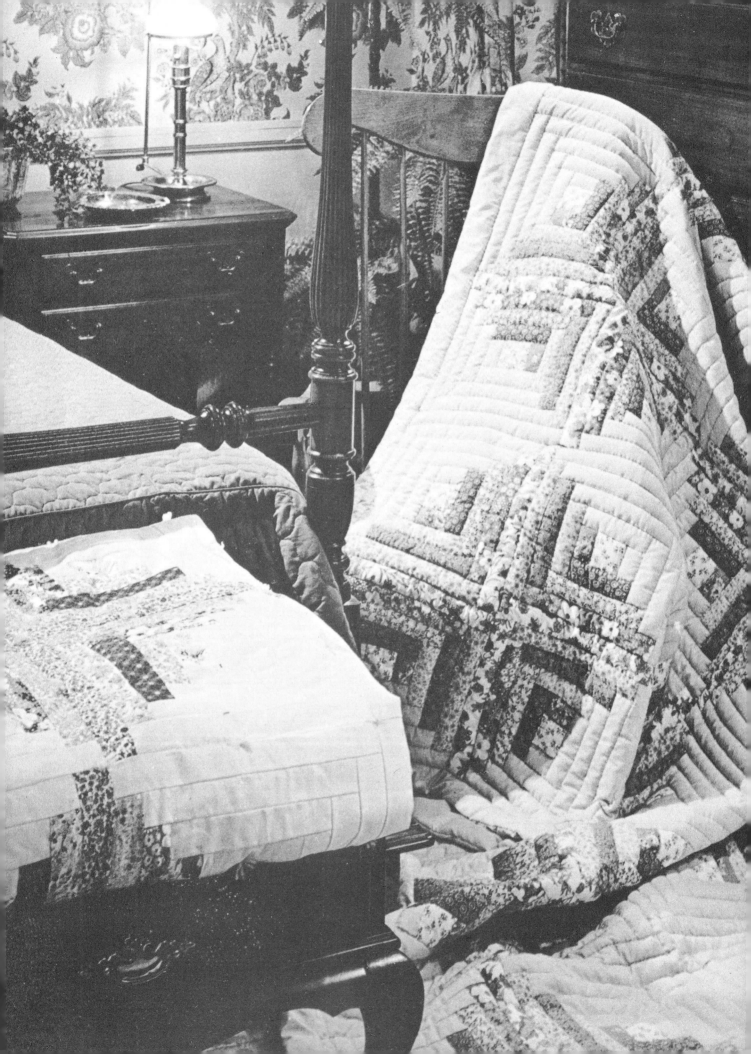

PATCHWORK QUILT

My grandmother's quilt
  was a royal affair,
Bright as her memory,
  soft as her hair.
Though patches were patterned
  like chords on a spinet,
There was more than color
  of calico in it.

The green-and-gold plaid
  was your Dad's kilted skirt;
He was wild as a colt,
  but handsome and pert.
The piece like a fire
  was a red flannel shirt.

The navy blue
  has a border of black,
I stitched it that way
  for your brave Uncle Jack;
He ran off to sea
  and never came back.

A shirtwaist of challis
  teenagers won't wear,
But your grandfather liked it.
  He said at the fair
That my eyes were a match
  for the brown of his mare.

My grandmother's smile
  was honey on bread,
As she hand-sewed gay patches
  and dreams with a thread.
She blinked back a tear;
  her head took a tilt.
"It's more like an album,"
  she said, "than a quilt."

Louis J. Sanker

Once upon a memory
Someone wiped away a tear,
Held me close and loved me,
Thank you, Mother, dear.

May Hensler Mueller

Fly Softly, My Love

First you smile,
    and press her to your heart,
And the closeness is etched deeply forever;
But all too soon,
    with even that first step,
She begins a path of her own.
Only she can follow it;
    can find her own true way.
So you laugh with her,
    and love her gently away from you,
Encouraging her search,
    knowing your heart is always open to her.
You give her the roots of home, of love,
Yet you show her the wings of peace.
    Fly softly, my love
    My gentle, gentle dove.

Shari Style

In the Firelight

The fire upon the hearth is low,
  And there is stillness everywhere,
While, like winged spirits, here and there
  The firelight shadows fluttering go.
And as the shadows round me creep,
  A childish treble breaks the gloom,
And softly, from a further room,
  Comes "Now I lay me down to sleep."

And somehow, with that little prayer
  And that sweet treble in my ears,
My thoughts go back to distant years
  And linger with a loved one there.

And as I hear my child's Amen,
  My mother's faith comes back to me;
Crouched at her side I seem to be,
  And Mother holds my hands again.

Oh, for an hour in that dear place!
  Oh, for the peace of that dear time!
Oh, for that childish trust sublime!
  Oh, for a glimpse of Mother's face!
Yet, as the shadows round me creep,
  I do not seem to be alone,
Sweet magic of that treble tone
  And "Now I lay me down to sleep"!

Eugene Field

Tucking the Baby In

The dark-fringed eyelids slowly close
  On eyes serene, and deep;
Upon my breast my own sweet child
  Has gently dropped to sleep,
I kiss his soft and dimpled cheek,
  I kiss his rounded chin,
Then lay him on his little bed,
  And tuck my baby in.

How fair and innocent he lies;
  Like some small angel strayed,
His face still warmed by God's own smile
  That slumbers unafraid;
Or like some new embodied soul,
  Still pure from taint of sin—
My thoughts are reverent as I stoop
  To tuck my baby in.

What toil must stain these tiny hands
  That now lie still and white?
What shadows creep across the face
  That shines with morning light?

Curtis May

The Fingers
of Love

The fingers of love sew and bake,
Plant spring flowers and gently rake,
   Scrub a cookie-strewn kitchen floor,
   Open wide a nursery door,
Trill in chords a musical scale,
Guide a young hand to pound a nail,
   Turn the pages of books to read,
   Point the path for velocipede,
Pull with glee a little red cart.
Fingers of love moved by the heart
   Smooth the pillows of nighttime fear
   And brush away a small child's tear.

Shirley Nadine Harkins

My Mother's Hands

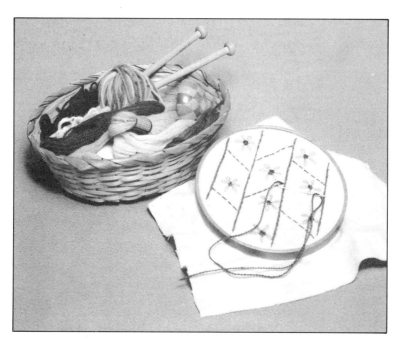

My mother's hands were never still,
So many varied chores had she.
How comforting when I was ill,
They soothed my brow and steadied me.

Sometimes, when I am by myself,
Memories take me back to when
Her hands filled every oven shelf
With kneaded bread to bake, and then

To other chores, in our back yard
She plucked her garden's yield each day.
No task to her seemed dull or hard,
For each she did in loving way.

My mother's hands were never still,
They scoured and sewed till late each night.
I see her yet, I always will,
Queen of the home she made happy and bright.

Dorothy Bettencourt Elfstrom

Photograph Opposite
Alpha Photo Associates

Bouquet for Mother

All blooms are a flower
To a child you see;
And a child is as joyful
As he can be,

When he picks the bloom
That we thoughtlessly call
A weed, for he loves them
And gathers them all.

A bouquet for mother
In a tight-fisted clutch,
Limp and fast fading,
Not looking like much,

But to the young eyes
Beholding them bright,
They're lovely and beautiful
For Mother's delight.

Ethel Bailey Bunch

Photograph Opposite
WASHINGTON
Ed Cooper

Overleaf
WASHINGTON
Ed Cooper

Daisies

At evening when I go to bed
I see the stars shine overhead;
They are the little daisies white
That dot the meadow of the night.

And often while I'm dreaming so,
Across the sky the moon will go;
It is a lady, sweet and fair,
Who comes to gather daisies there.

For, when at morning I arise,
There's not a star left in the skies;
She's picked them all and dropped them down
Into the meadows of the town.

Frank Dempster Sherman

Photograph Opposite
Fred Sieb

For the mother is and must be,
whether she knows it or not,
the greatest, strongest and most lasting teacher
her children have.

Hannah Whitall Smith

What More?

Phyllis C. Michael

Could any mother wish for more?
I stand beside my open door
And look out on a world so grand,
And yet confused on ev'ry hand;
I wonder what the future holds
For you, my child, as the scene unfolds,
And in my heart there is just one prayer,
"May God go with you everywhere."

There are many things I could wish for you,
And some of them might even come true;
But I won't build castles that crumble and fall,
For that would never do at all.
Dreams are made of such gossamer stuff
That they vanish at even the slightest puff;
And so, in my heart there's just one prayer,
"May God go with you everywhere."

Flower of Virtue

Throughout the United States, carnations have symbolized the spirit behind Mother's Day. This tradition began on the first Mother's Day in 1908, when Ann Jarvis, the woman primarily responsible for establishing the day honoring mothers, furnished everyone in her local church with one of the spring flowers. She chose the white carnations to symbolize purity, as well as the other virtues she associated with mothers, such as sweetness, beauty, charity, faithfulness, and enduring love. In later years, however, those whose mothers still lived wore brilliant red carnations, whereas those whose mothers had passed away wore white carnations in loving remembrance.

A White Carnation

To a Mother's love I witness bear,
    By this fragrant flower I proudly wear.
'Tis snowy white to some who see,
    But it's a brilliant, crimson red to me.
Although her lips I cannot kiss,
    I feel her presence. Though I miss
Her loving touch, her tender care,
    She's always with me, everywhere.

Virgil Judson Temple

Photograph Opposite
Robert Cushman Hayes

MOTHER'S DAY

SUNDAY, MAY 10, 1908

The Second Sabbath of May is Mother's.
A Day for Loyal Sons and Daughters
to Especially Honor Their Mothers.

This day is set apart for loyal sons and daughters of Andrews M. E. Sunday School of Grafton, West Virginia, to especially honor their faithful and good mothers.

Everybody is invited, but to mothers we give a special invitation, and special honor; with a desire in our mind to prove and show, that although we sometimes neglect and forget them, that away down deep in our hearts, we love them, and wish by this day to give pleasure to all. "To put gladness into the heart of a good mother is real religion."

The Purpose of the Day.

To revive dormant filial love and gratitude.

To be a home tie for the absent.

To obliterate family estrangement.

To create a bond of brotherhood through the wearing of the floral badge.

To make us better children by getting us closer to the hearts of our good mothers.

To brighten the lives of good mothers.

To have them know that we appreciate them, though we do not show it as often as we ought.

Each one present will be given a white carnation; mothers will be given two, in memory of the day.

These five hundred carnations are given by a loyal, loving daughter in honor and sacred memory of her good and faithful mother, Mrs. Ann M. Jarvis, who worked faithfully and earnestly for twenty long years, as an earnest teacher in our Sunday School, who only a few years ago departed to that better world to reap the reward of her labors here.

Everyone is asked to wear this flower.

The white carnation is preferred, because it may be thought to typify some of the virtues of motherhood; for instance its whiteness stands for purity, its lasting qualities, faithfulness; its fragrance, love; its wide field of growth, charity; its form, beauty.

Do not all of us who feel we have or had the best mother who ever lived, think of her as pure, faithful, loving; forgiving and beautiful?

Looking Backward.

Few of us, if any, are so fortunate as to be able to look back to any time in our lives with regret, because we were too dutiful, gentle, kind, and generous to our good mothers. On the contrary, most of us if not all, have heartaches, when too late, we wish we were more loving, more dutiful, more thoughtful in every way, to give pleasure, when we could; so that this day is intended to bring to our mind a more active thought, to make the lives of our mothers happier and brighter, and to see where we can improve on the past.

Very often our good mothers hunger and yearn for the loving thoughts which every true mother cherishes. Often a good mother's life is filled with emptiness: because of love never shown, and letters from the absent son and daughter that never come. And yet no man or woman is too poor or too busy to remember this devoted parent.

Mother's Day is to remind us of our duty before it is too late.

This day is intended that we may make new resolutions for a more active thought to our dear mothers. By words, gifts, acts of affection, and in every way possible, give her pleasure, and make her heart glad every day, and constantly keep in memory Mother's Day; when you made this resolution, lest you forget and neglect your dear mother, if absent from home write her often, tell her of a few of her noble good qualities and how you love her.

"A mother's love is new every day."

God bless our faithful good mothers.

L.L. Loar
Superintender of Andrews M. E. Sunday School, Grafton, W. Va.

Little Miss Make-Believe

Little Miss Make-Believe, dressed up so gay
With Mother's long dress and high heels at play.
Such finery, fluffery, feathery clothes
That little Miss Make-Believe charmingly shows:
Long gloves to the elbow where pocketbook swings,
A hat that is covered with bird's snow-white wings;
A veil that hangs softly to cover the face,
A bow of bright ribbon and pieces of lace.
Smelling sweet of perfume, all made up with care,
A stole on her arm which she loves to wear.
A pink parasol, the outfit complete
As little Miss Make-Believe strolls down the street.
Little Miss Make-Believe dressed up so gay,
Are you some great model or movie star gay?
"Oh, no! I'm my Mother; it's fun to be she."
"Then thank you, my daughter, for you flatter me."

Esther Lloyd Dauber

Love Is the Bond of Generations

A Grandma and a Little Boy

Between the grandma and the little boy,
    There is a precious bond of blood and race,
That skips the years between and makes them one;
    The same blue eyes, the little heart-shaped face,
Between these two there is a special glow,
    That only little boys and grandmas know.

They sit together in the family pew,
    He finds the hymn and hands the book to her,
Inches a little closer to her side;
    Before her dim old eyes the pages blur,
And yet they sing together tenderly,
    The old familiar hymn, "Abide with me."

He sits within the circle of her arm,
    And drowses gently while the preacher prays
She pats him with her thin, old, tired hands,
    Her gentle thoughts go back to bygone days,
When this one's father in the selfsame pew,
    Wiggled and squirmed as small boys ever do.

And so the grandma and the little boy,
    Are only two of all the valiant band,
Who come and go like shadows on a screen,
    The upright sons and daughters of our land,
Who hold within their hands the precious keys,
    That mark the progress of the centuries.

Edna.Jaques

A Tribute to Grandma

Each Mother's Day we pause to pay
    Due honor to our mothers.
We all agree our own dear mom
    Is best above all others.

        There are tributes read to mother,
            And those to daughters, too,
        But what about our grandma,
            She deserves a line or two.

No one plays with children,
    Quite the way that grandmas do,
With her family all grown up now,
    She has lots of time for you.

She's the favorite baby-sitter;
    Her baking's the best in town;
And when Susie wants a doll dress,
    Grandma never lets her down.

        So let's think about our grandma,
            As we celebrate this year;
        She is someone very special
            We will always hold most dear.

                        Mary Jane Herbert

Woman Deeply Loved

To see and watch her is to know
That she is deeply loved. Her face
Reflects this. Love has left its trace
In her serenity, the glow
Of deep contentment in her eyes,
Her joyous laugh, the cheerful way
She goes about her work each day.
Love haloes women, beautifies
The plainest face, for more than bread
To every woman is the knowing
She is cherished; keeps her glowing
With confidence, affection-fed:
Her happiness so much a part
Of love, enshrined within her heart.

Velma West Sykes

Strength and dignity are her clothing;
  And she laugheth at the time to come.
She openeth her mouth to wisdom;
  And the law of kindness is in her tongue.

She looketh well to the ways of her household,
  And eateth not the bread of idleness;
Her children rise up and call her blessed,
  Her husband, also, and he praiseth her, saying:

"Many daughters have done virtuously,
  But thou excelleth them all."

Proverbs 31:25-29

THE FAMILY ALBUM

I well remember as a girl
I'd crawl on Grandma's lap
To see her family album, and
There by the hour we sat!

We'd see Aunt Jennie, Uncle Charles,
And little cousin, Sue,
Who's really very grown-up now,
In fact, she's married, too!

We'd see Grandpa as just a boy;
A dog he held so tight
(This was his playmate many years,
A wiggly, friendly sight!)

I saw Grandma as just a girl,
Her collar stiff and high;
I wondered, did all of the girls
Look so demure and shy?

And what I really wouldn't give
To go back to the day
When I could sit on Grandma's lap
And see those pictures gay!

Georgia B. Adams

God Dwell with Us

God bless this home with love and peace;
May wholesome laughter never cease
To fill each room and hall.

If time should bring one passing tear,
Let there be friends, true friends, in here
To help and comfort all.

Give faith and hope, enough and to spare;
Give time for earnest thought and prayer,
Let thy love bless each wall.

May those who enter find life a bit brighter,
May burdens be lifted, may hearts seem lighter,
Because they paid us a call.

Phyllis C. Michael

otograph Opposite
MHERST, N. H.
Fred Sieb

Mothering Sunday

It is the day of all the year,
Of all the year the one day
When I shall see my mother dear
And bring her cheer,
   A-mothering on Sunday.

In nineteenth-century England an ecclesiastical order established the fourth Sunday in Lent as Mothering Sunday. On this holiday young men and women who labored in the cities as servants, apprentices, and factory workers returned home with gifts, bouquets of wild flowers, cakes, and occasionally a newly acquired sweetheart for family approval. As the children performed the household duties and prepared the dinner, the mothers were free to attend the morning church service.

The children also made an elaborately and skillfully decorated simnel cake. Similar to a fruitcake, a simnel cake had a rich filling of cherries, plums, raisins, cinnamon, and many other fruits and spices. Topped with a crust of flour, water, and saffron, the cake was boiled in a cloth, glazed with egg, and finally baked. The resulting pastry was so large and hard-crusted that one mother actually mistook it for a wooden footstool. Once past the crust, however, the family savored a deliciously spicy treat.

The name "simnel" is derived from the Latin *simila*, a fine wheaten flour. A curious folk legend, however, offers another explanation for the origin of this name. According to lore, a woman and her husband were making a special cake for their children. Disagreeing over the method of cooking the cake, they finally compromised by first boiling and then baking it. In the same spirit, they named the cake with a combination of both their names, Simon and Nelly.

Although the observance of Mothering Sunday gradually faded out, the custom was revived in the United States and renamed Mother's Day. Today, as at the time of the industrial revolution, this day in honor of mothers serves to reunite and preserve the family.

Beverly Rae Wiersum

Simnel Cake (Modern Version)

Cream together 1 cup (½ lb.) butter with 1 cup sugar. Sift 2 cups flour with 1 tsp. grated nutmeg, 1 tsp. ground cinnamon, 1 tsp. ground ginger, ½ tsp. salt, and 2 tsp. baking powder. With 2½ cups raisins and 2 cups currants mix ¾ cup cherries and ¾ cup chopped candied peel. Beat 4 eggs, add 2 tbsp. milk and 1 tsp. vanilla. Work beaten eggs into creamed mixture. Gradually add half the flour, then add all the fruit, finally mix in remainder of flour (mixture should be fairly stiff). Line a 9-inch tin with several thicknesses of wax paper. Put half the mixture into the tin, smoothing the top evenly. Over this place a half-inch round of almond paste. Add remainder of mixture, smooth top, and bake in a slow oven (325°) for 4 hours.

When cake is cool, cut out another round of almond paste exactly the size of cake. Cut a three-inch round from the center and place the ring of paste on top of the cake. Form a number of small balls or eggs (11 is the traditional number) with the remainder of the paste and lay these at intervals on the ring of almond paste. Brush with beaten egg and place in a hot oven (500°) for 2½ minutes, or until paste is slightly brown. When cold, fill the center of the cake with glacé frosting. When this is set, use a pastry tube to decorate the cake with an appropriate greeting.

Glacé Frosting for Simnel Cake

Combine 1 cup sieved confectioners' sugar, 2 tbsp. water and 1 tbsp. strained lemon juice in the top of a double boiler. Stir over hot water until sugar is melted. The frosting should be only warm. While still warm, pour over cake.

It is the day of all the year,
Of all the year the one day
When I shall see my mother dear,
And bring her cheer,
  A-mothering on Sunday.

So I'll put on my Sunday coat,
And in my hat a feather,
And get the lines I writ by rote,
With many a note
That I've a-strung together.
  A-mothering on Sunday.

It is the day of all the year,
Of all the year the one day;
And here come I, my mother dear,
To bring you cheer.
  A-mothering on Sunday.

George Hare Leonard

Maternal Song

How can I tell of a mother's worth?
By a song of the all-sustaining earth;
The earth that watches young plants rise
With arms outstretched to the distant skies;

The earth that gives them zeal to grow,
But keeps their eager roots in tow;
That urges them to stand up proud,
Sustains them when their heads are bowed,

And strengthens them to face again
The thrusts of wind and hail and rain,
So they may bloom, bear fruit and seed
To meet the hungering, tired world's need.

I sing of the kindly, nurturing earth
To tell of a mother's priceless worth.

Sudie Stuart Hager

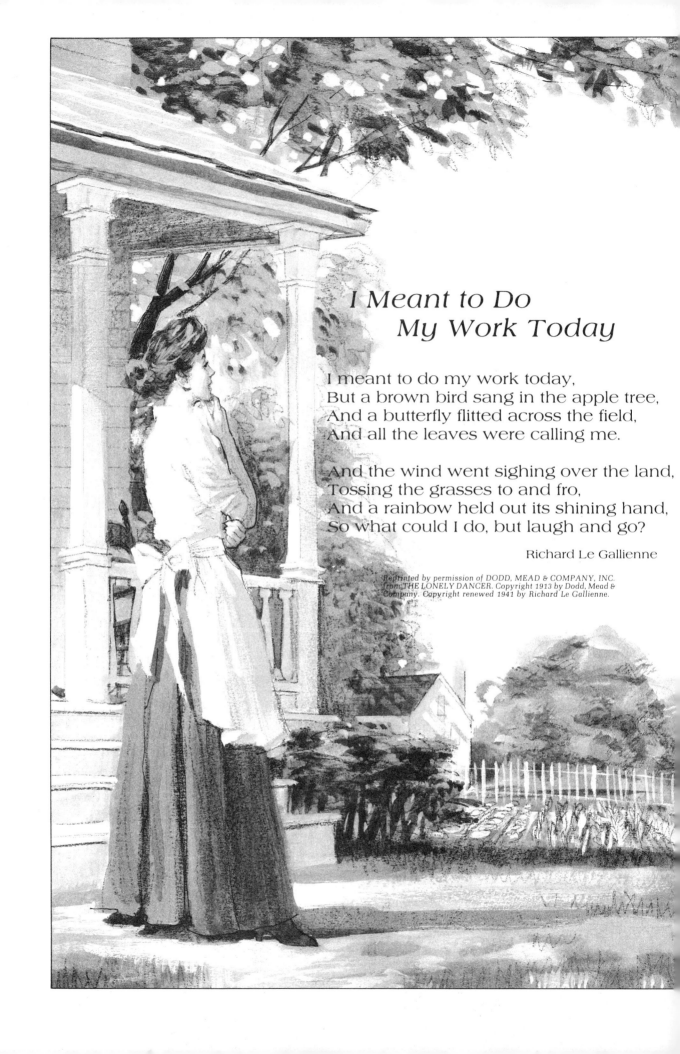

I Meant to Do
My Work Today

I meant to do my work today,
But a brown bird sang in the apple tree,
And a butterfly flitted across the field,
And all the leaves were calling me.

And the wind went sighing over the land,
Tossing the grasses to and fro,
And a rainbow held out its shining hand,
So what could I do, but laugh and go?

Richard Le Gallienne

Reprinted by permission of DODD, MEAD & COMPANY, INC.
from THE LONELY DANCER. Copyright 1913 by Dodd, Mead &
Company. Copyright renewed 1941 by Richard Le Gallienne.

In Quest of Happiness

Today I'll go in search of lovely things;
The golden marvel of a flicker's wings,
The tender beauty of a new-leafed tree—
These I have passed, perhaps, and failed to see.

Today I'll find in every face I meet
Something untarnished, something brave and sweet;
I shall be slow to censure, swift to praise,
Generous with my love this day of days.

Today I'll go in quest of happiness,
Glad for the sun's warm kiss, the wind's caress,
Glad for the faith that keeps me free and strong,
Glad for the breath of praise, the gift of song.

Today I will accept what God has planned,
And leave tomorrow in his gracious hand;
All my yesterdays he swept away,
And I rejoice. Today is God's own day!

Bonnie J. McClelland

Hymn for
Mother's Day

We pray that thou wilt greatly bless
Our mothers on this day,
With treasures from thy heavenly store
That cannot pass away.

The love that shields our infancy,
The love that guides our youth,
That shows the wonders of thy law,
The glories of thy truth.

O God, we thank thee for the gifts
That come from thee alone,
And chiefly for that mother's love
Which is so like thine own;

We pray that sons and daughters all
May ever loyal be,
And may our mothers' prayers fulfill
By truly serving thee.

Emily S. Coit

Living

Thelma Williamson

O wondrous life that lets me see
A sky of blue, a golden tree!
A small child's happy little face,
Bright flowers in a lovely vase;
That lets me hear a song so sweet,
Gay people, laughing, down the street;
That lets me feel a tiny hand
Nestled in mine, and understand
The thrill of fun, the ache of pain,
The warmth of sun, the wet of rain;
That bestows love and lets me give
And then say:
"Thank you, God, I live!"

Reflections

Vivian Volk

The budding trees, the oak, the elm,
The lilac bearing shoots,
The bridal wreath, the climbing rose,
    Fruits of awakened roots.

Our hearts have taught our eyes to see,
These proud displays of spring,
Blind to the homely beauty that
    A violet can bring.

And it's the same with life and love,
We reach with empty arms,
And search for what we can't attain,
    Ignorant of the charms

Found in the warmth of a handclasp,
In the echoing of songs,
Within the peace of hallowed walls,
    This is where love belongs.

Seek not the bud that promises
A flowering supreme,
First pick the blossoms at your feet
    And therein, find a dream.

The Masterpiece

Paintings are moments
    Held captive in time,
Telling their story
    Without prose or rhyme.

Give us that perfect
    Object d'art,
Treasure for millions,
    Both near and far;
Beauty to lift our
    Thoughts up above,
Paint us a mother,
    Portrait of love.
Find the right canvas,
    Look for the best,
Mount it and prime it,
    Then let it rest.
Study the masters,
    Only truth lasts.
Show how the present
    Transcends the past.
Use for your background
    Soft shades of blue,
Even at this stage
    Love must show through.
Sketch your design
    Universal in scope,

Show for mankind both
    Promise and hope.
Touch it with colors
    Living can bring,
Spread on some laughter;
    Make the heart sing!
Remember the children,
    That girl or boy,
Brush in some heataches,
    Cover with joy.
Capture the feeling
    The world understands:
Love that will listen,
    Hands touching hands.
Bring out the highlights,
    Treasures that shine;
Times that seem hardest
    Tend to refine.

Mark it eternal,
    Touch it with prayer.
When you have finished
    Sign with a flair.
Show it with other
    Great works of art,
Portrait of Mother
    Lives in the heart!

Alice Leedy Mason

Painting Opposite
MOTHER AND CHILD
by Mary Cassatt
American 1844-1926
Cincinnati Art Museum
John J. Emery Endowment

Beatitudes for Mothers

Blessed are the mothers of yesterday, for their memories shall be called beautiful and beneficent. They are like flowers growing by sunken gardens and beside still water and in green fields, for they are like soft winds that blow with peace and love on wistful wings.

Blessed are the mothers of today, for they have the keeping of tomorrow in their hands and in their hearts; and the destiny of nations, hearts and homes.

Blessed are the mothers of tomorrow, for they have been summoned to a great and heroic hour. For they shall be called the mothers of men who shall make miracles of human life. The mothers of tomorrow shall breed a race of giants who handle lightning as a little thing, and make the clouds and thunder obey their wills; blessed are the mothers of tomorrow.

Blessed are the mothers of scientists and statesmen; of laborers and poets; of preachers and prophets; of teachers and dreamers; for dreams and visions and prophecies and the glow and glory of creation is born in the hearts of mothers.

Blessed are the mothers, for they are conservers of the human race.

Blessed are the mothers, for they taught barbarian ancestors to grow grains and build shelters.

Blessed are the mothers of the world, for they have conserved the spiritual things of life for the sake of their children.

Blessed are the mothers of the earth, for they have combined the practical and the spiritual into one workable way of human life. They have darned little stockings, mended little dresses, washed little faces, and have pointed little eyes to the stars and little souls to eternal things.

Blessed are the mothers!

William L. Stidger

On the following six pages
we are presenting a selection
from Mother's Day Ideals 1948.

Mother's
ideals
VOL. 3

Tuckin' The Babies In

By Edward Coulou Craig

It's the very last thing I do at night
    When I'm tired from giving my best,
    All in the house is silent and at rest
But the timid cricket who is not in sight.
I go to the babies' room to see if
    They are asleep, and if all is well
And always I find they're resting,
    But the covers are quite pell-mell.

So I straighten each rumpled fold
    And turn a tousled blond head,
Over soft tender skins I spread
The blankets to keep out the cold;
A sigh in repose—now maybe she's dreaming
Of a tame bear licking her chin,
Or riding a pony who does clever tricks—
    While I'm tuckin' the babies in.

My spirit mother has come from afar
    To nurse my babies so fast asleep,
    Their souls through strange lands sweep
When sleep thus leaves the door ajar.
Speak softly now, on tiptoe tread
    For the spirit canoe is very thin
Which glides with mother on emerald lakes
    While I'm tuckin' the babies in.

MOTHER'S DAY

Frank Carleton Nelson

Sweet Motherhood, this day is thine,
Today we bow to thee,
Hearts filled with love and thankfulness
For thy sweet memory.

*Upon the throne of every mind
You sit as queen today,
Our tender love and reverence
At thy dear feet we lay.*

For Motherhood the world today
Would offer up a prayer,
And the emblem of this land of ours
Floats proudly in the air.

*In honor, too, a flower is worn,
A token of our love,
A gift from God for Motherhood,
And blest by Him above.*

Throughout the years that are to come
May this day ever be,
A day to honor Motherhood
Oh, God, we ask of Thee.

Mother's Songs

The songs my Mother sang to me,
Are ringing still across the years,
And woven with each melody
Are Mother's smiles and Mother's tears.

My Mother's words are set in gold,
They are my gems of memory,
My soul had vision to behold
Each sparkling phrase she gave to me.

My Mother's eyes are pools so deep,
That their reflection, shining still,
Shall comfort me in my last sleep,
And bless me on the far, green hill.

My Mother's arms! My Mother's kiss!
My life has not been lived in vain,
If, in a better world than this,
I am her little child again.

Our sincere thanks to the unknown author.

MOTHER WITH INFANT SON
By Sir JOSHUA REYNOLDS (1723-1792)
Original in The Wallace Collection, London

Thinking of You

Barton Rees Pogue

I'll be thinking of you all the day, dear one,
Thinking all day of you,
Longing all day for the touch of your hand,
Wishing the whole day through
That I might sit there, in the place of prayer,
With you and your friends and the flowers they wear,
And with those who have lost, gladly share
The love of a mother like you.

I want to be there with you, dear one,
I want to be there with you,
I'll be charging the times for bringing me here
So far removed from you;
But the miles can't blur the vision I see
Of one who's dearer each day to me,
Who doesn't need pray that she may be
A mother fond and true.

Remember the days I picked marigolds
And brought them home to you?
Remember the violets I dug and set
There by the house for you?
Those little blue flowers have wandered away
From the corner where I put them that day,
But they're spreading a message, and it's this they say:
"Your child is in love with you."

"It's a man-made day," someone has said,
"And commercial through and through!"
But I wouldn't miss joining my hands with those
Paying honor to mothers like you!
My greatest hope in this happy hour—
That my heart shall always wear a flower,
That we both may live so I may shower
More of my love on you!

A hundred singing things I find to say
to greet you lavishly upon this day;
a litany of years parade their thanks
with memory of graduated ranks:
the love felt in the fog of babyhood,
the later years of being understood,
the sunshine days, the days with overcast,
the thousand times, their shape lost in the past,
when, grown but groping, counsel led the way.
Where is the pauper eloquence to say
the gratitude, so sluggish in its birth,
for days, that tally up a lifetime's worth?

The words come somehow badly in the end.
Now with abbreviated song I send
a spring-swept greeting meant to say
quite simply, "Happy Mother's Day."

Patricia Martin Zens

Dear Mom,
We hope you know that
you're very special to us!
We will always love you
and each day the love grows even
stronger.
To our No 1st Mom of
the year.
Love Forever,
Butch, Kathy & Girls

Coming in Carefree Days Ideals—

A colorful feature story on the Petrified Forest
. . . the pictorial artistry of Josef Muench . . .
Ideals' Best-Loved Poet James Whitcomb Riley
. . . Pages from the Past, Travel Ideals, 1954 . . .
a charming excerpt from a children's classic
Toby Tyler or Ten Weeks with a Circus . . . plus
poetry and prose beautifully illustrated to share
with you the carefree days of summer.

ACKNOWLEDGMENTS

THE FAMILY ALBUM by Georgia B. Adams. From THE SILVER FLUTE by Georgia
B. Adams. Copyright © 1968 by Georgia B. Adams. Published by Dorrance & Company.
ALL I ASK; GOD DWELL WITH US; THE MOTHER OF MANY; MOTHER'S
HELPER; MY WISH FOR YOU; TO MOTHER-IN-LAW; WHAT MORE? by Phyllis C.
Michael. Copyright 1963 by Phyllis C. Michael in POEMS FOR MOTHERS. A
MOTHER'S PART. Copyright 1964 by Phyllis C. Michael in POEMS FROM MY
HEART. All Phyllis C. Michael poems used by permission. BEATITUDES FOR
MOTHERS by William L. Stidger. Used through courtesy of William S. Hyland.
LIVING by Thelma Williamson. Used with permission of the author. Our sincere
thanks to the following authors whose addresses we were unable to locate: Bonnie J.
McClelland for IN QUEST OF HAPPINESS; Louis J. Sanker for PATCHWORK
QUILT; Velma West Sykes for WOMAN DEEPLY LOVED; Virgil Judson for A WHITE
CARNATION.

Additional Photo Credits: Front cover, Robert Cushman Hayes. Inside front cover, H.
Armstrong Roberts. Inside back cover, H. Armstrong Roberts. Back cover, Jewel
Craig.